hen

Henne

rooster

Hahn

chick

Küken

duckling

Entenküken

turkey

Truthahn

donkey

Esel

swan

Schwan

frog

Frosch

racoon

Waschbär

bear

Bär

squirrel

Eichhörnchen

fly

Fliege

ladybug

Marienkäfer

worm

Wurm

snail

Schnecke

slug

Nacktschnecke

bee

Biene

spider

Spinne

beetle

Käfer

dragonfly

Libelle

lion

Löwe

zebra

Zebra

giraffe

Giraffe

rhinoceros

Nashorn

snake

Schlange

mosquito

Mücke

sea turtle

meeresschildkröte

hippopotamus

Nilpferd

alligator

alligator

crocodile

Krokodil

shark

Hai

walrus

Walross

penguin

Pinguin

polar bear

Eisbär

seal

Robbe

starfish

Seestern

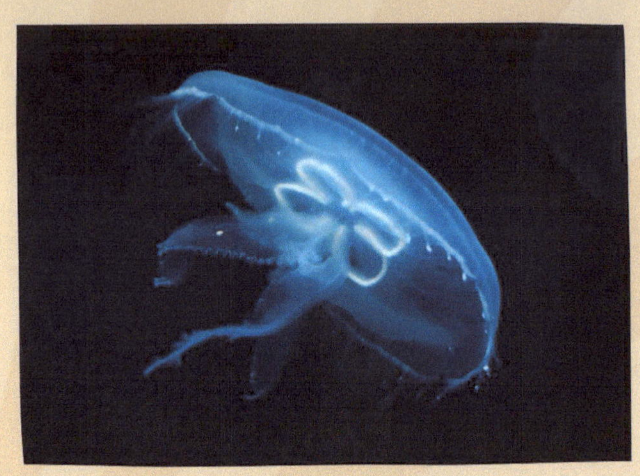

jellyfish

Qualle

seashells

Muscheln

feather

Feder

11

eleven

elf

12

twelve

zwölf

13

thirteen

dreizehn

14

fourteen

Vierzehn

15	**16**
fifteen	sixteen
fünfzehn	sechzehn

17	**18**
seventeen	eighteen
siebzehn	achtzehn

19

nineteen

neunzehn

20

twenty

zwanzig

heart

Herz

oval

oval

arrow

Pfeil

crescent

Halbmond

curve

Kurve

spiral

Spirale

cross

Kreuz

zigzag

Zickzack

rainbow
Regenbogen

dark colors
dunkle Farben

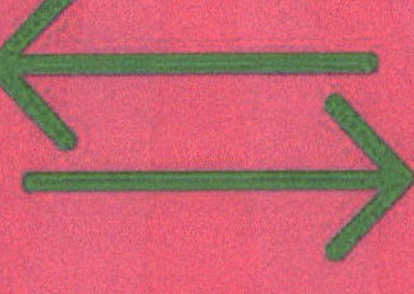

light colors
helle Farben

dots

Punkte

line

Linie

short

klein

tall

groß

 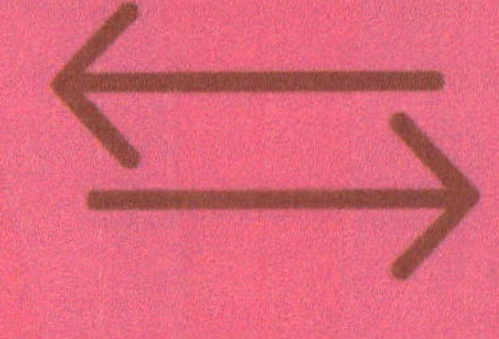 

a little

ein wenig

a lot

viel

full

voll

empty

leer

curly hair

lockiges Haar

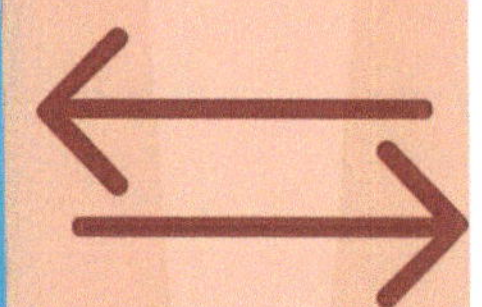

straight hair

glattes Haar

accept

akzeptieren

refuse

verweigern

identical

identisch

different

unterschiedlich

dry

trocken

wet

nass

toys

Spielzeuge

blocks

Blöcke

ball

Ball

robots

Roboter

tongue

Zunge

nose

Nase

hair

Haare

moustache

Schnurrbart

fingers

Finger

arm

Arm

knee

Knie

elbow

Ellbogen

smile

lächeln

kiss

küssen

cry

weinen

pain

Schmerz

body

Körper

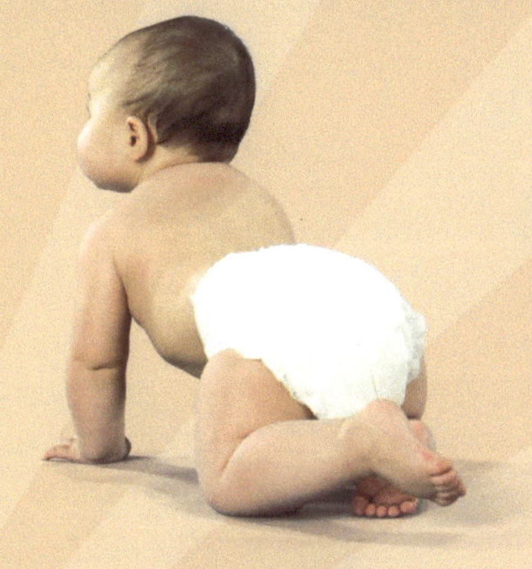

back

Rücken

pacifier

Schnuller

high chair

Hochstuhl

soap

Seife

toothbrush

Zahnbürste

towel

Handtuch

potty

Töpfchen

ring

Ring

bracelet

Armband

necklace

Halskette

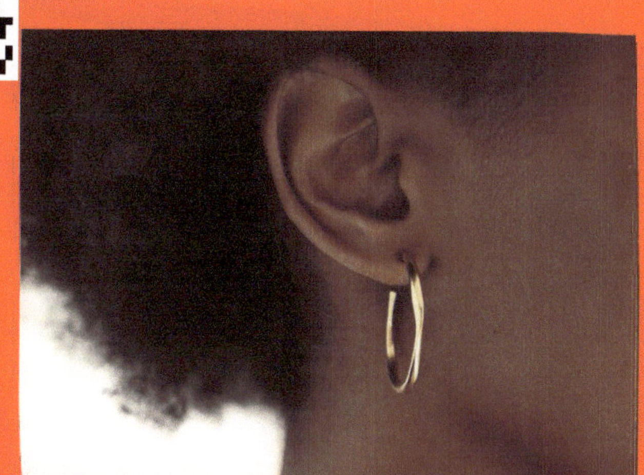

earring

Ohrring

chocolate

Schokolade

popcorn

Popcorn

jam

Marmelade

toast

Toast

honey

Honig

butter

Butter

bread

Brot

ice cream

Eis

semolina

Grieß

rice

Reis

pasta

Pasta

soup

Suppe

milk

Milch

water

Wasser

juice

Saft

kiwi

Kiwi

raspberry

Himbeere

grapefruit

Grapefruit

melon

Melone

plum

Pflaume

apricot

Aprikose

pomegranate

Granatapfel

fig

Feige

blueberry

Heidelbeere

cranberry

Preiselbeere

persimmon

Kaki

lychee

Litschi

fruits

Früchte

vegetables

Gemüse

avocado

Avocado

green bean

grüne Bohne

broccoli

Brokkoli

eggplant

Aubergine

peas

Erbsen

bell pepper

Paprika

beet

Rote Beete

lettuce

Salat

endive

Endivie

artichoke

Artischocke

leek

Lauch

onion

Zwiebel

garlic

Knoblauch

ginger

Ingwer

walnuts

Walnüsse

almond

Mandel

pistachio

Pistazie

cashew

Cashew